OWL & CAT

RAMADAN IS...

WORDS & PICTURES
BY EMMA APPLE

For everyone who celebrates Ramadan and all of our friends and family who wonder what Ramadan is...

For Blake, Dylan and Liam.

Books by Emma Apple – Chicago IL USA

First Edition.

ISBN-13: 978-0692717950

www.emmaapple.com

OWL & CAT

RAMADAN IS...

Ramadan is a whole month, every year, when Muslims fast (fasting means you don't eat or drink) from sunrise until sunset.

Ramadan is a special time, celebrated with many traditions and a spirit of generosity and gratitude.

Ramadan is...

Spotting the crescent moon!

Ramadan is...

Eating suhoor
(the pre dawn meal).

Ramadan is...

The month of the Qur'an.

Ramadan is...

Remembering Allah.

Ramadan is...

Being grateful.

Ramadan is...

Special food!

Ramadan is...

Watching the sunrise.

Ramadan is...

Going to the mosque!

Ramadan is...

Praying together.

Ramadan is...

Family and friends.

Ramadan is...

Delicious dates!

Ramadan is...

Staying up late!

Ramadan is...

Taking naps.

(Shhh!)

Ramadan is...

Cooking together!

Ramadan is...

Decorating!

Ramadan is...

Sharing meals.

Ramadan is...

Crafting!

Ramadan is...

Learning!

Ramadan is...

Family time.

Ramadan is...

Making new friends!

Ramadan is...

Lights and lanterns!

Ramadan is...

Being patient!

Ramadan is...

Eating iftar
(breaking the fast).

Ramadan is...

Giving charity.

Ramadan is...

Forgiveness.

Ramadan is...

Fun with friends!

Ramadan is...

Shopping!

Ramadan is...

An accomplishment!

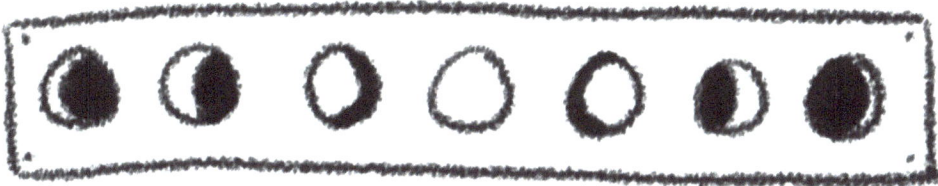

Ramadan is...

Gifts!

Ramadan is...

New clothes for Eid!

After Ramadan...

IT'S EID!

THE

OWL & CAT

SERIES

Loosely based on the characters from the timeless children's poem *The Owl and The Pussycat* by Edward Lear. Owl & Cat, Muslim picture books help children learn about the concepts of Friendship, Family and Acceptance, with humor and an appeal that crosses the lines of culture and religion. **Perfect for multicultural homes, classrooms, and libraries.**

ABOUT THE AUTHOR

Emma Apple is a best selling Islamic Children's author-illustrator.

Her debut as an author-illustrator, *How Big Is Allah?* was independently published in 2014 and quickly reached #1 in the Amazon Islamic Children's category. The follow up books in the Children's First Questions series, *How Does Allah Look?* and *Where Is Allah?* were released in 2015 and 2016 respectively.

More from Emma Apple:
emmaapple.com